Grace Filled Days

A Year of Scripture and Reflection

JACLYN *jb* BUFTON

———— ♥ ———— ♥ ————

To Stacy, whose unwavering faith and boundless grace inspired the pages of this book. Your light shines brightly in the lives of those around you, reminding us all of the power of love, kindness, and the beauty of grace-filled days. Thank you for being a source of inspiration and encouragement on my journey.

———— ♥ ———— ♥ ————

———— ♥ ———— ♥ ————

Grace Filled Days: A Year of Scripture and Reflection
invites readers to start each day with a fresh perspective, cultivating
a heart of gratitude and a spirit of kindness as they embrace
the transformative power of God's Word.

———— ♥ ———— ♥ ————

Table of Contents

Getting the Most Out of This Book

These verses have been carefully chosen to accompany you each day, serving as a source of inspiration and a reminder of the beauty and grace that can be found in everyday moments. At the beginning of each month, take a moment to center yourself and focus on the prayer prompt, allowing it to guide your thoughts and intentions as you embrace the theme of the month. Then, each day, as you read the scripture, allow yourself to pause and truly engage with its message. Reflect on what the words mean to you personally—consider how they resonate with your experiences, aspirations, and challenges.

As you contemplate the teachings within these verses, think about practical ways to incorporate their wisdom into your daily life. Ask yourself how the themes of love, compassion, and understanding can guide your thoughts and influence your actions. Consider the impact these messages might have on your relationships with others—how can you embody positivity and grace in your interactions, fostering an environment of kindness and support?

At the end of each month, you'll find a dedicated page for your reflections. This space is an opportunity to jot down your thoughts, insights, and experiences related to the scriptures you've encountered. Use it to track your growth, celebrate your progress, and recognize the changes in your mindset and behavior. Reflecting on these verses can deepen your understanding and help you stay aligned with your intentions, creating a meaningful journey of personal development.

Let this practice be a way to cultivate a habit of mindfulness and gratitude, ensuring that each day is filled with intention and purpose. By engaging with these verses and your reflections, you're not only enriching your own life but also empowering yourself to spread positivity and grace to those around you. Embrace the transformative power of these scriptures as they guide you on your journey, and watch how they shape your days and the lives of others.

———— ♥ ———— ♥ ————

January

Embracing New Beginnings

———— ♥ ———— ♥ ————

Prayer Prompt:
"Lord, help me to embrace
this new season with an
open heart. Show me the
opportunities before me and
guide my steps as I begin
anew."

Embracing New Beginnings

As we step into January, I look forward to embracing the theme of new beginnings with you, celebrating the fresh start this month brings. Jeremiah 29:11 reminds us that God has beautiful plans for each of us—plans filled with hope and a future. This is a perfect time to reflect on His intentions and trust that they are for our good.

In this season of renewal, let's remember that we can do all things through Christ who strengthens us (Philippians 4:13). As women, we often juggle many roles, but with His power, we are equipped to face any challenge with grace.

Though there may be moments of difficulty, Psalm 30:5 encourages us that "weeping may last through the night, but joy comes with the morning." No matter what struggles we face, there is always hope for brighter days ahead. Isaiah 41:10 reassures us, "Don't be afraid, for I am with you." His presence is our source of strength and courage.

In the midst of life's storms, let's take refuge in the Lord, our strong fortress (Proverbs 18:10). Isaiah 43:2 promises that when we go through deep waters, we will not drown; He is right there with us, guiding us through every challenge.

This month, let's pray for an abundance of joy and peace as Romans 15:13 states. May our trust in Him fill our hearts completely, reminding us that we are not alone in our journeys. As we interact with one another, Ephesians 4:32 encourages us to practice kindness and forgiveness, creating a nurturing community where we can grow together.

As we reflect on our identities, 2 Corinthians 5:17 reminds us that in Christ, we are made new. Let go of any burdens from the past and embrace the new life He offers. Psalm 118:24 calls us to rejoice in each day the Lord has made, embracing the beauty and opportunities that come with it.

Let's shine our light brightly, as Matthew 5:16 encourages us, allowing our good deeds to reflect the love of our heavenly Father. Trust in the Lord with all your heart (Proverbs 3:5-6), and remember to cast all your worries on Him, for He cares deeply for you (1 Peter 5:7).

As we cultivate our hopes and dreams, let's not grow weary in doing good. Galatians 6:9 assures us that at just the right time, we will reap a harvest of blessings if we don't give up. And as we take delight in the Lord (Psalm 37:4), we'll discover that He truly fulfills our heart's desires.

May January be a month of transformation, where we embrace new beginnings, trust in His plans, and support one another in our journeys. Together, let's step boldly into the future, filled with hope and joy!

1. Jeremiah 29:11 - "For I know the plans I have for you, says the Lord. They are plans for good and not for disaster, to give you a future and a hope."

2. Philippians 4:13 - "For I can do everything through Christ, who gives me strength."

3. Psalm 30:5 - "Weeping may last through the night, but joy comes with the morning."

4. Isaiah 41:10 - "Don't be afraid, for I am with you. Don't be discouraged, for I am your God."

5. Proverbs 18:10 - "The name of the Lord is a strong fortress; the godly run to him and are safe."

6. Isaiah 43:2 - "When you go through deep waters, I will be with you. When you go through rivers of difficulty, you will not drown."

7. Romans 15:13 - "I pray that God, the source of hope, will fill you completely with joy and peace because you trust in him."

8. Ephesians 4:32 - "Instead, be kind to each other, tenderhearted, forgiving one another, just as God through Christ has forgiven you."

9. 2 Corinthians 5:17 - "This means that anyone who belongs to Christ has become a new person. The old life is gone; a new life has begun!"

10. Psalm 118:24 - "This is the day the Lord has made. We will rejoice and be glad in it."

11. Matthew 5:16 - "In the same way, let your good deeds shine out for all to see, so that everyone will praise your heavenly Father."

12. Proverbs 3:5-6 - "Trust in the Lord with all your heart; do not depend on your own understanding. Seek his will in all you do, and he will show you which path to take."

13. 1 Peter 5:7 - "Give all your worries and cares to God, for he cares about you."

14. Colossians 3:2 - "Think about the things of heaven, not the things of earth."

15. Galatians 6:9 - "So let's not get tired of doing what is good. At just the right time we will reap a harvest of blessing if we don't give up."

16. Psalm 37:4 - "Take delight in the Lord, and he will give you your heart's desires."

17. Romans 12:12 - "Rejoice in our confident hope. Be patient in trouble, and keep on praying."

18. John 16:33 - "I have told you all this so that you may have peace in me. Here on earth you will have many trials and sorrows. But take heart, because I have overcome the world!"

19. Isaiah 40:31 - "But those who trust in the Lord will find new strength. They will soar high on wings like eagles."

20. James 1:2-3 - "Dear brothers and sisters, when troubles of any kind come your way, consider it an opportunity for great joy."

21. Psalm 139:14 - "Thank you for making me so wonderfully complex! Your workmanship is marvelous—how well I know it."

22. Ephesians 2:8-9 - "God saved you by his grace when you believed. And you can't take credit for this; it is a gift from God."

23. Philippians 4:6-7 - "Don't worry about anything; instead, pray about everything. Tell God what you need, and thank him for all he has done."

24. Proverbs 17:22 - "A cheerful heart is good medicine, but a broken spirit saps a person's strength."

25. Romans 8:28 - "And we know that God causes everything to work together for the good of those who love God and are called according to his purpose for them."

26. Psalm 46:1 - "God is our refuge and strength, always ready to help in times of trouble."

27. Matthew 11:28 - "Come to me, all of you who are weary and carry heavy burdens, and I will give you rest."

28. Psalm 23:1 - "The Lord is my shepherd; I have all that I need."

29. 2 Timothy 1:7 - "For God has not given us a spirit of fear and timidity, but of power, love, and self-discipline."

30. 1 John 4:19 - "We love each other because he loved us first."

31. Lamentations 3:22-23 - "The faithful love of the Lord never ends! His mercies never cease. Great is his faithfulness; his mercies begin afresh each morning."

Take a moment to reflect on this months scripture. What message or messages resonate with you? How can you apply these teaching in your life today? Consider its impact on your thoughts, actions, and relationships.

February

Embracing New Growth

Prayer Prompt:
"Father, as I continue to embrace new beginnings, remind me to let go of the past. Fill me with hope and anticipation for the future you have in store."

February

Embracing New Growth

As we step into February, let's focus on the theme of embracing growth. This month offers us a chance to reflect on our journeys as women and recognize the incredible potential for personal and spiritual development. Philippians 1:6 assures us that God is actively at work within us, continuing the good work He has begun. No matter where you find yourself, trust that you are on a path of growth.

Let's take this time to release any burdens that hold us back, as Hebrews 12:1 encourages us to do. It's important to identify what might be slowing us down and to focus on moving forward. Matthew 6:34 reminds us to concentrate on today's challenges, not tomorrow's worries. Each step you take is an opportunity for growth, so let's approach each day with intention.

Psalm 55:22 invites us to hand over our worries to the Lord, who cares for us deeply. As we face life's ups and downs, let's lift each other up with kind words that encourage and empower (Proverbs 16:24). Together, we can overcome negativity by actively choosing to do good (Romans 12:21).

In our daily endeavors, let's commit to working with passion and purpose, as if we are serving the Lord (Colossians 3:23). Ephesians 3:20 reminds us that God can achieve more through us than we can imagine. Trust that He is nurturing your growth and leading you toward fulfilling your potential.

As we look ahead, Isaiah 43:18-19 encourages us to embrace what God is doing in our lives right now. Forget past limitations and focus on the new opportunities He is creating. In times of difficulty, remember that God provides strength to the weak (Isaiah 40:29) and peace in every situation (2 Thessalonians 3:16).

This February, let's cultivate gratitude and joy in our hearts (1 Thessalonians 5:16-18) and seek wisdom in our decisions (Proverbs 4:7). Allow His word to guide you, illuminating your path (Psalm 119:105) and leading you toward growth.

As we gather in community, let's support each other in our growth journeys. Remember, if God is for us, who can stand against us? (Romans 8:31). Embrace this month as a time to cultivate your potential and celebrate the growth that lies ahead!

———— ♥ ———— ♥ ————

1. Philippians 1:6 - "And I am certain that God, who began the good work within you, will continue his work until it is finally finished on the day when Christ Jesus returns."

2. Hebrews 12:1 - "Therefore, since we are surrounded by such a huge crowd of witnesses to the life of faith, let us strip off every weight that slows us down."

3. Matthew 6:34 - "So don't worry about tomorrow, for tomorrow will bring its own worries. Today's trouble is enough for today."

4. Psalm 55:22 - "Give your burdens to the Lord, and he will take care of you."

5. Romans 12:21 - "Don't let evil conquer you, but conquer evil by doing good."

6. Colossians 3:23 - "Work willingly at whatever you do, as though you were working for the Lord rather than for people."

7. Ephesians 3:20 - "Now all glory to God, who is able, through his mighty power at work within us, to accomplish infinitely more than we might ask or think."

8. Psalm 121:1-2 - "I look up to the mountains—does my help come from there? My help comes from the Lord, who made heaven and earth!"

9. Proverbs 16:24 - "Kind words are like honey—sweet to the soul and healthy for the body."

10. Isaiah 61:3 - "To all who mourn in Israel, he will give a crown of beauty for ashes, a joyous blessing instead of mourning."

11. 1 Corinthians 10:13 - "The temptations in your life are no different from what others experience. And God is faithful. He will not allow the temptation to be more than you can stand."

12. Romans 8:31 - "What shall we say about such wonderful things as these? If God is for us, who can ever be against us?"

13. Philippians 4:8 - "And now, dear brothers and sisters, one final thing. Fix your thoughts on what is true, and honorable, and right, and pure, and lovely, and admirable."

14. Psalm 119:105 - "Your word is a lamp to guide my feet and a light for my path."

15. 1 Thessalonians 5:16-18 - "Always be joyful. Never stop praying. Be thankful in all circumstances, for this is God's will for you who belong to Christ Jesus."

16. Psalm 119:114 - "You are my refuge and my shield; your word is my source of hope."

17. Isaiah 43:18-19 - "But forget all that—it is nothing compared to what I am going to do. For I am about to do something new. See, I have already begun! Do you not see it?"

18. 2 Thessalonians 3:16 - "Now may the Lord of peace himself give you peace at all times and in every situation."

19. Colossians 2:6-7 - "And now, just as you accepted Christ Jesus as your Lord, you must continue to follow him. Let your roots grow down into him, and let your lives be built on him."

20. Psalm 119:50 - "Your promise revives me; it comforts me in all my troubles."

21. Isaiah 40:29 - "He gives power to the weak and strength to the powerless."

22. Romans 15:5-6 - "May God, who gives this patience and encouragement, help you live in complete harmony with each other, as is fitting for followers of Christ Jesus."

23. Proverbs 4:7 - "Getting wisdom is the most important thing you can do! And whatever else you do, develop good judgment."

24. Philippians 4:7 - "Then you will experience God's peace, which exceeds anything we can understand."

25. Psalm 34:4 - "I prayed to the Lord, and he answered me. He freed me from all my fears."

26. Hebrews 13:5-6 - "Don't love money; be satisfied with what you have. For God has said, 'I will never fail you. I will never abandon you.'"

27. Matthew 19:26 - "Jesus looked at them intently and said, 'Humanly speaking, it is impossible. But with God everything is possible.'"

28. 1 Thessalonians 4:13-14 - "And now, dear brothers and sisters, we want you to know what will happen to the Christians who have died so you will not grieve like people who have no hope."

Reflections

Take a moment to reflect on this months scripture. What message or messages resonate with you? How can you apply these teaching in your life today? Consider its impact on your thoughts, actions, and relationships.

March

Embracing Our Divine Pupose

———— ♥ ———— ♥ ————

Prayer Prompt:
"God, reveal to me the
unique purpose you've
designed for my life. Help
me to walk confidently in it
and to trust your plan for
my journey."

March

Embracing Our Divine Purpose

As we enter March, let's focus on the theme of embracing our divine purpose. This month, we are called to recognize and celebrate the unique gifts and callings God has placed within each of us. We are reminded in Ephesians 2:10 that we are God's masterpiece, created to do good works that He planned long ago. Take this opportunity to reflect on what it means to live out that purpose every day.

This month, consider how you can align your daily actions with your divine calling. Whether it's through acts of kindness, sharing your talents, or simply being present for someone in need, each small step contributes to a greater impact. Remember, as Isaiah 58:9 assures us, when we call on the Lord, He is always there to guide and support us. Trust that you are not walking this journey alone.

In moments of challenge or doubt, lean on the assurance found in Psalm 121:7-8: "The Lord keeps you from all harm and watches over your life." Embrace the knowledge that you are cared for, and that your purpose is intertwined with His loving plan. As women, we have the unique ability to nurture and uplift those around us. This month, let's inspire each other to step boldly into our roles, knowing that we are supported by a loving community.

Let this be a time to deepen your relationship with God. Spend time in prayer and reflection, inviting Him to reveal more about your purpose. Philippians 3:20 reminds us that we are citizens of heaven, where Christ reigns, and our lives have eternal significance. As you seek Him, trust that He will illuminate your path and strengthen your resolve.

Finally, take time at the end of the month to journal your reflections on how you've embraced your purpose and how it has shaped your interactions and experiences. Let's celebrate the beauty of being uniquely crafted by God, filled with potential to do good in the world. Remember, you are not only a vessel of His love but also a beacon of hope for others. May this March be a month of clarity, purpose, and joy as we walk confidently in the light of His love!

1. Ephesians 2:10 - "For we are God's masterpiece. He has created us anew in Christ Jesus, so we can do the good things he planned for us long ago."

2. Isaiah 58:9 - "Then when you call, the Lord will answer. 'Yes, I am here,' he will quickly reply."

3. James 1:12 - "God blesses those who patiently endure testing and temptation. Afterward they will receive the crown of life that God has promised to those who love him."

4. Philippians 2:3-4 - "Don't be selfish; don't try to impress others. Be humble, thinking of others as better than yourselves. Don't look out only for your own interests, but take an interest in others, too."

5. Psalm 23:4 - "Even when I walk through the darkest valley, I will not be afraid, for you are close beside me."

6. Proverbs 15:13 - "A glad heart makes a happy face; a broken heart crushes the spirit."

7. Romans 8:1 - "So now there is no condemnation for those who belong to Christ Jesus."

8. 1 Peter 3:15 - "Instead, you must worship Christ as Lord of your life. And if someone asks about your Christian hope, always be ready to explain it."

9. 2 Corinthians 1:3-4 - "All praise to God, the Father of our Lord Jesus Christ. God is our merciful Father and the source of all comfort. He comforts us in all our troubles."

10. Psalm 91:1-2 - "Those who live in the secret place of the Most High will find rest in the shadow of the Almighty. This I declare about the Lord: He alone is my refuge, my place of safety; he is my God, and I trust him."

11. Proverbs 18:15 - "Intelligent people are always ready to learn. Their ears are open for knowledge."

12. Philippians 3:20 - "But we are citizens of heaven, where the Lord Jesus Christ lives. And we are eagerly waiting for him to return as our Savior."

13. Ephesians 6:12 - "For we are not fighting against flesh-and-blood enemies, but against evil rulers and authorities of the unseen world, against mighty powers in this dark world, and against evil spirits in the heavenly places."

14. Colossians 1:27 - "For God wanted them to know that the riches and glory of Christ are for you Gentiles, too. And this is the secret: Christ lives in you. This gives you assurance of sharing his glory."

15. Psalm 121:7-8 - "The Lord keeps you from all harm and watches over your life. The Lord keeps watch over you as you come and go, both now and forever."

16. James 1:17 - "Whatever is good and perfect is a gift coming down to us from God our Father, who created all the lights in the heavens."

17. Isaiah 40:31 - "But those who trust in the Lord will find new strength. They will soar high on wings like eagles."

18. Romans 4:20-21 - "Abraham never wavered in believing God's promise. In fact, his faith grew stronger, and in this he brought glory to God. He was fully convinced that God is able to do whatever he promises."

19. Psalm 138:8 - "The Lord will work out his plans for my life—for your faithful love, O Lord, endures forever. Don't abandon me, for you made me."

March

20. Philippians 1:9-10 - "I pray that your love will overflow more and more, and that you will keep on growing in knowledge and understanding."

21. Psalm 63:1 - "O God, you are my God; I earnestly search for you. My soul thirsts for you; my whole body longs for you in this parched and weary land where there is no water."

22. 1 Corinthians 15:58 - "So, my dear brothers and sisters, be strong and immovable. Always work enthusiastically for the Lord, for you know that nothing you do for the Lord is ever useless."

23. Revelation 21:4 - "He will wipe every tear from their eyes, and there will be no more death or sorrow or crying or pain. All these things are gone forever."

24. **Psalm 56:3** - "But when I am afraid, I will put my trust in you."

25. 1 Peter 5:10 - "In his kindness God called you to share in his eternal glory by means of Christ Jesus. So after you have suffered a little while, he will restore, support, and strengthen you, and he will place you on a firm foundation."

26. Psalm 100:4-5 - "Enter his gates with thanksgiving; go into his courts with praise. Give thanks to him and praise his name. For the Lord is good. His unfailing love continues forever, and his faithfulness continues to each generation."

27. Isaiah 26:3 - "You will keep in perfect peace all who trust in you, all whose thoughts are fixed on you!"

28. Hebrews 4:16 - "So let us come boldly to the throne of our gracious God. There we will receive his mercy, and we will find grace to help us when we need it most."

March

29. James 4:8 - "Come close to God, and God will come close to you. Wash your hands, you sinners; purify your hearts, for your loyalty is divided between God and the world."

30. Philippians 4:19 - "And this same God who takes care of me will supply all your needs from his glorious riches, which have been given to us in Christ Jesus."

31. Psalm 107:1 - "Give thanks to the Lord, for he is good! His faithful love endures forever."

Take a moment to reflect on this months scripture. What message or messages resonate with you? How can you apply these teaching in your life today? Consider its impact on your thoughts, actions, and relationships.

April

Embracing Peace and Community

Prayer Prompt:
"Lord, grant me the wisdom
to foster peace in my
relationships. Help me to
contribute positively to my
community and to be a
source of love and support
for others."

Embracing Peace and Community

As we enter April, let's focus on the theme of embracing peace and community. This month is a reminder of the importance of cultivating peace within ourselves and fostering harmony with those around us. Colossians 3:15 encourages us to let the peace of Christ rule in our hearts, creating a foundation of gratitude and unity among us.

In times of trouble, remember Psalm 119:50: "Your promise revives me." God's promises are a source of comfort and strength, especially when we face challenges. When we feel overwhelmed, we can lean on the truth of Isaiah 41:10, which reassures us that we are never alone—God is with us, guiding us through our fears.

As we build our community, Romans 15:5-6 reminds us to live in harmony, offering patience and encouragement to one another. This is especially vital as we navigate our diverse paths. Let's strive to think of others as better than ourselves (Philippians 2:3-4), creating an atmosphere where everyone feels valued and supported.

This month, let's also seek wisdom in our decisions (Proverbs 4:7). Understanding the importance of good judgment helps us to contribute positively to our community. Philippians 4:7 promises that when we embrace God's peace, it surpasses all understanding—allowing us to face life's challenges with grace.

When fear and anxiety arise, turn to Psalm 34:4, where David shares how he sought the Lord and found freedom from his fears. Let this be a reminder that we can always call on God, who is faithful (2 Timothy 2:13), and who will never abandon us (Hebrews 13:5-6).

This April, let's encourage one another to embrace the community we have and to build each other up in faith. With God, everything is possible (Matthew 19:26), and as we come together in unity, we reflect the love of Christ to the world. Embrace this month as a time to deepen relationships, cultivate peace, and trust in the God who brings us together!

April

1. Psalm 37:23-24 - "The Lord directs the steps of the godly. He delights in every detail of their lives. Though they stumble, they will never fall, for the Lord holds them by the hand."

2. Matthew 7 - "Keep on asking, and you will receive what you ask for. Keep on seeking, and you will find. Keep on knocking, and the door will be opened to you."

3. Isaiah 40:29 - "He gives power to the weak and strength to the powerless."

4. Psalm 119:32 - "I will run in the path of your commands, for you have set my heart free."

5. Proverbs 3:6 - "Seek his will in all you do, and he will show you which path to take."

6. Romans 5:1-2 - "Therefore, since we have been made right in God's sight by faith, we have peace with God because of what Jesus Christ our Lord has done for us."

7. Colossians 3:15 - "And let the peace that comes from Christ rule in your hearts. For as members of one body you are called to live in peace. And always be thankful."

8. Psalm 119:50 - "Your promise revives me; it comforts me in all my troubles."

9. 2 Timothy 2:13 - "If we are unfaithful, he remains faithful, for he cannot deny who he is."

10. Isaiah 41:10 - "Don't be afraid, for I am with you. Don't be discouraged, for I am your God."

11. Romans 15:5-6 - "May God, who gives this patience and encouragement, help you live in complete harmony with each other, as is fitting for followers of Christ Jesus."

12. Proverbs 4:7 - "Getting wisdom is the most important thing you can do! And whatever else you do, develop good judgment."

13. Philippians 4:7 - "Then you will experience God's peace, which exceeds anything we can understand."

14. Psalm 34:4 - "I prayed to the Lord, and he answered me. He freed me from all my fears."

15. Hebrews 13:5-6 - "Don't love money; be satisfied with what you have. For God has said, 'I will never fail you. I will never abandon you.'"

16. Matthew 19:26 - "Jesus looked at them intently and said, 'Humanly speaking, it is impossible. But with God everything is possible.'"

17. Thessalonians 4:13-14 - "And now, dear brothers and sisters, we want you to know what will happen to the Christians who have died so you will not grieve like people who have no hope."

18. Ephesians 2:10 - "For we are God's masterpiece. He has created us anew in Christ Jesus, so we can do the good things he planned for us long ago."

19. Isaiah 58:9 - "Then when you call, the Lord will answer. 'Yes, I am here,' he will quickly reply."

20. James 1:12 - "God blesses those who patiently endure testing and temptation. Afterward they will receive the crown of life that God has promised to those who love him."

21. Philippians 2:3-4 - "Don't be selfish; don't try to impress others. Be humble, thinking of others as better than yourselves."

22. Psalm 23:4 - "Even when I walk through the darkest valley, I will not be afraid, for you are close beside me."

23. Proverbs 15:13 - "A glad heart makes a happy face; a broken heart crushes the spirit."

24. Romans 8:1 - "So now there is no condemnation for those who belong to Christ Jesus."

25. 1 Peter 3:15 - "Instead, you must worship Christ as Lord of your life. And if someone asks about your Christian hope, always be ready to explain it."

26. 2 Corinthians 1:3-4 - "All praise to God, the Father of our Lord Jesus Christ. God is our merciful Father and the source of all comfort. He comforts us in all our troubles."

27. Psalm 91:1-2 - "Those who live in the secret place of the Most High will find rest in the shadow of the Almighty."

28. Colossians 1:27 - "For God wanted them to know that the riches and glory of Christ are for you Gentiles, too. And this is the secret: Christ lives in you. This gives you assurance of sharing his glory."

29. Philippians 3:20 - "But we are citizens of heaven, where the Lord Jesus Christ lives. And we are eagerly waiting for him to return as our Savior."

30. Ephesians 6:12 - "For we are not fighting against flesh-and-blood enemies, but against evil rulers and authorities of the unseen world, against mighty powers in this dark world, and against evil spirits in the heavenly places."

Take a moment to reflect on this months scripture. What message or messages resonate with you? How can you apply these teaching in your life today? Consider its impact on your thoughts, actions, and relationships.

———— ♥ ———— ♥ ————

May

Pursuing Wisdom and Strength

———— ♥ ———— ♥ ————

Prayer Prompt:
"Dear God, fill me with your
wisdom and strength as I
navigate challenges. Help me
to seek your guidance in
every decision I make."

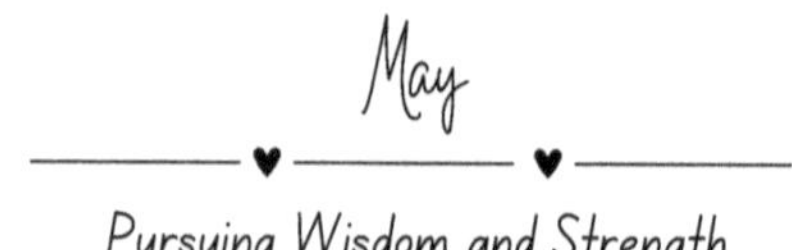

May

Pursuing Wisdom and Strength

As we welcome the month of May, let's focus on the theme of pursuing wisdom and strength. This month is an invitation for women to seek knowledge and empowerment in our daily lives, embracing the gifts God has given us and the strength He provides.

Proverbs 18:15 reminds us that "Intelligent people are always ready to learn." Let this be a month of curiosity and exploration. Seek out opportunities to grow in wisdom, whether through reading, engaging in meaningful conversations, or reflecting on your life experiences. Each moment is a chance to learn something new, and as we grow in knowledge, we can share that insight with others, uplifting those around us.

Psalm 121:7-8 reassures us that "The Lord keeps you from all harm and watches over your life." Trust in His protective presence as you pursue your goals this month. When challenges arise, remember that you have the strength of God behind you, as Isaiah 40:29 states, "He gives power to the weak and strength to the powerless." You are never alone in your journey; draw on His strength to overcome any obstacles you face.

As you navigate this month, take time to reflect on the promises of God. In moments of doubt or fear, lean into the comfort of Psalm 119:50: "Your promise revives me." Allow His words to refresh your spirit and instill confidence in your heart. Surround yourself with reminders of His faithfulness and be grateful for the good gifts He has placed in your life, as mentioned in James 1:17.

This May, let's not only seek wisdom for ourselves but also encourage one another. In Philippians 2:3-4, we're called to consider others' interests alongside our own. Reach out to fellow women, share your insights, and support each other in your individual journeys. Together, we can create a community that thrives on collective wisdom and strength.

At the end of the month, take a moment to journal your reflections on what you've learned, how you've felt God's strength in your life, and the ways you've been able to encourage others. Embrace this season of pursuit—of wisdom, of strength, and of heartfelt connection.

May this month be filled with discovery and empowerment as we seek knowledge, support one another, and walk confidently in the strength that God provides!

1. Proverbs 18:15 - "Intelligent people are always ready to learn. Their ears are open for knowledge."

2. Psalm 121:7-8 - "The Lord keeps you from all harm and watches over your life. The Lord keeps watch over you as you come and go, both now and forever."

3. James 1:17 - "Whatever is good and perfect is a gift coming down to us from God our Father, who created all the lights in the heavens."

4. Isaiah 40:29 - "He gives power to the weak and strength to the powerless."

5. Psalm 119:32 - "I will run in the path of your commands, for you have set my heart free."

6. Proverbs 3:6 - "Seek his will in all you do, and he will show you which path to take."

7. Romans 5:1-2 - "Therefore, since we have been made right in God's sight by faith, we have peace with God because of what Jesus Christ our Lord has done for us."

8. Colossians 3:15 - "And let the peace that comes from Christ rule in your hearts. For as members of one body you are called to live in peace. And always be thankful."

9. Psalm 119:50 - "Your promise revives me; it comforts me in all my troubles."

10. 2 Timothy 2:13 - "If we are unfaithful, he remains faithful, for he cannot deny who he is."

11. Isaiah 41:10 - "Don't be afraid, for I am with you. Don't be discouraged, for I am your God."

12. Romans 15:5-6 - "May God, who gives this patience and encouragement, help you live in complete harmony with each other, as is fitting for followers of Christ Jesus."

13. Proverbs 4:7 - "Getting wisdom is the most important thing you can do! And whatever else you do, develop good judgment."

14. Philippians 4:7 - "Then you will experience God's peace, which exceeds anything we can understand."

15. Psalm 34:4 - "I prayed to the Lord, and he answered me. He freed me from all my fears."

16. Hebrews 13:5-6 - "Don't love money; be satisfied with what you have. For God has said, 'I will never fail you. I will never abandon you.'"

17. Matthew 19:26 - "Jesus looked at them intently and said, 'Humanly speaking, it is impossible. But with God everything is possible.'"

18. 1 Thessalonians 4:13-14 - "And now, dear brothers and sisters, we want you to know what will happen to the Christians who have died so you will not grieve like people who have no hope."

19. Ephesians 2:10 - "For we are God's masterpiece. He has created us anew in Christ Jesus, so we can do the good things he planned for us long ago."

20. Isaiah 58:9 - "Then when you call, the Lord will answer. 'Yes, I am here,' he will quickly reply."

21. James 1:12 - "God blesses those who patiently endure testing and temptation. Afterward they will receive the crown of life that God has promised to those who love him."

22. Philippians 2:3-4 - "Don't be selfish; don't try to impress others. Be humble, thinking of others as better than yourselves."

23. Psalm 23:4 - "Even when I walk through the darkest valley, I will not be afraid, for you are close beside me."

23. Proverbs 15:13 - "A glad heart makes a happy face; a broken heart crushes the spirit."

24. Romans 8:1 - "So now there is no condemnation for those who belong to Christ Jesus."

25. 1 Peter 3:15 - "Instead, you must worship Christ as Lord of your life. And if someone asks about your Christian hope, always be ready to explain it."

26. 2 Corinthians 1:3-4 - "All praise to God, the Father of our Lord Jesus Christ. God is our merciful Father and the source of all comfort. He comforts us in all our troubles."

27. Psalm 91:1-2 - "Those who live in the secret place of the Most High will find rest in the shadow of the Almighty."

28. Colossians 1:27 - "For God wanted them to know that the riches and glory of Christ are for you Gentiles, too. And this is the secret: Christ lives in you. This gives you assurance of sharing his glory."

29. Philippians 3:20 - "But we are citizens of heaven, where the Lord Jesus Christ lives. And we are eagerly waiting for him to return as our Savior."

30. Ephesians 6:12 - "For we are not fighting against flesh-and-blood enemies, but against evil rulers and authorities of the unseen world, against mighty powers in this dark world, and against evil spirits in the heavenly places."

31. Proverbs 18:15 - "Intelligent people are always ready to learn. Their ears are open for knowledge."

Reflections

Take a moment to reflect on this months scripture. What message or messages resonate with you? How can you apply these teaching in your life today? Consider its impact on your thoughts, actions, and relationships.

————— ♥ ————— ♥ —————

June

Living in Faith and Assurance

————— ♥ ————— ♥ —————

Prayer Prompt:
"Heavenly Father, help me to
live each day in faith,
trusting your promises.
Strengthen my assurance in
your presence and provision
in my life."

June

─────── ♥ ─────── ♥ ───────

Living in Faith and Assurance

As we step into June, let's focus on the theme of living in faith and assurance. This month is a reminder for women to anchor ourselves in the unwavering promises of God and to boldly trust in His plans for our lives.

Psalm 121:7-8 assures us that "The Lord keeps you from all harm and watches over your life." Take comfort in knowing that God is actively watching over you in every step you take. His presence is a constant source of strength and safety, guiding you through both the ordinary and the extraordinary moments of life.

In the spirit of faith, let's embrace the truth found in James 1:17: "Whatever is good and perfect is a gift coming down to us from God." This month, make it a goal to recognize and celebrate the good gifts in your life, no matter how small. Gratitude opens our hearts and shifts our perspectives, allowing us to see God's hand in every situation.

Isaiah 41:10 encourages us not to fear, reminding us that God is with us. When doubts creep in or challenges arise, hold fast to this promise. Trust in His faithfulness, knowing that He provides power to the weak and strength to the powerless (Isaiah 40:29). Each time you feel overwhelmed, remember that you can call on Him for support.

As you navigate your days, let Psalm 119:32 inspire you to run joyfully in the path God has set for you. Seek His will in all you do (Proverbs 3:6), and be open to the adventures and opportunities He places in your path. Whether it's pursuing a new project, fostering relationships, or simply taking time for self-care, trust that He will guide you toward His perfect plans.

This month, let's also commit to lifting each other up in faith. Romans 15:5-6 calls us to live in harmony, encouraging one another in our journeys. Share your hopes, your fears, and your victories with your sisters in Christ, creating a supportive space where everyone can flourish in their faith.

June

At the end of June, take a moment to reflect on how God has shown His faithfulness in your life. Journal your experiences, prayers, and the ways you have seen His gifts unfold. Let this reflection deepen your assurance in His plans and remind you of the beautiful ways He works in your life.

May this month be filled with faith-filled moments, as we trust in God's goodness and walk confidently in the assurance that He is with us always!

June

1. Psalm 121:7-8 - "The Lord keeps you from all harm and watches over your life. The Lord keeps watch over you as you come and go, both now and forever."

2. James 1:17 - "Whatever is good and perfect is a gift coming down to us from God our Father, who created all the lights in the heavens."

3. Isaiah 40:29 - "He gives power to the weak and strength to the powerless."

4. Psalm 119:32 - "I will run in the path of your commands, for you have set my heart free."

5. Proverbs 3:6 - "Seek his will in all you do, and he will show you which path to take."

6. Romans 5:1-2 - "Therefore, since we have been made right in God's sight by faith, we have peace with God because of what Jesus Christ our Lord has done for us."

7. Colossians 3:15 - "And let the peace that comes from Christ rule in your hearts. For as members of one body you are called to live in peace. And always be thankful."

8. Psalm 119:50 - "Your promise revives me; it comforts me in all my troubles."

9. 2 Timothy 2:13 - "If we are unfaithful, he remains faithful, for he cannot deny who he is."

10. Isaiah 41:10 - "Don't be afraid, for I am with you. Don't be discouraged, for I am your God."

11. Romans 15:5-6 - "May God, who gives this patience and encouragement, help you live in complete harmony with each other, as is fitting for followers of Christ Jesus."

———————— ♥ ———————— ♥ ————————

12. Proverbs 4:7 - "Getting wisdom is the most important thing you can do! And whatever else you do, develop good judgment."

13. Philippians 4:7 - "Then you will experience God's peace, which exceeds anything we can understand."

14. Psalm 34:4 - "I prayed to the Lord, and he answered me. He freed me from all my fears."

15. Hebrews 13:5-6 - "Don't love money; be satisfied with what you have. For God has said, 'I will never fail you. I will never abandon you.'"

16. Matthew 19:26 - "Jesus looked at them intently and said, 'Humanly speaking, it is impossible. But with God everything is possible.'"

17. 1 Thessalonians 4:13-14 - "And now, dear brothers and sisters, we want you to know what will happen to the Christians who have died so you will not grieve like people who have no hope."

18. Ephesians 2:10 - "For we are God's masterpiece. He has created us anew in Christ Jesus, so we can do the good things he planned for us long ago."

19. Isaiah 58:9 - "Then when you call, the Lord will answer. 'Yes, I am here,' he will quickly reply."

20. James 1:12 - "God blesses those who patiently endure testing and temptation. Afterward they will receive the crown of life that God has promised to those who love him."

21. Philippians 2:3-4 - "Don't be selfish; don't try to impress others. Be humble, thinking of others as better than yourselves."

22. Psalm 23:4 - "Even when I walk through the darkest valley, I will not be afraid, for you are close beside me."

23. Proverbs 15:13 - "A glad heart makes a happy face; a broken heart crushes the spirit."

24. Romans 8:1 - "So now there is no condemnation for those who belong to Christ Jesus."

25. 1 Peter 3:15 - "Instead, you must worship Christ as Lord of your life. And if someone asks about your Christian hope, always be ready to explain it."

26. 2 Corinthians 1:3-4 - "All praise to God, the Father of our Lord Jesus Christ. God is our merciful Father and the source of all comfort. He comforts us in all our troubles."

27. Psalm 91:1-2 - "Those who live in the secret place of the Most High will find rest in the shadow of the Almighty."

28. Colossians 1:27 - "For God wanted them to know that the riches and glory of Christ are for you Gentiles, too. And this is the secret: Christ lives in you. This gives you assurance of sharing his glory."

29. Philippians 3:20 - "But we are citizens of heaven, where the Lord Jesus Christ lives. And we are eagerly waiting for him to return as our Savior."

30. Ephesians 6:12 - "For we are not fighting against flesh-and-blood enemies, but against evil rulers and authorities of the unseen world, against mighty powers in this dark world, and against evil spirits in the heavenly places."

Reflections

Take a moment to reflect on this months scripture. What message or messages resonate with you? How can you apply these teaching in your life today? Consider its impact on your thoughts, actions, and relationships.

July

Embracing Divine Gifts and Courage

Prayer Prompt:
"Lord, thank you for the
gifts you've bestowed upon
me. Help me to embrace
them boldly and to use them
for your glory and the
benefit of others."

July

♥ ─────── ♥ ───────

Embracing Divine Gifts and Courage

As we enter July, let's focus on the theme of embracing divine gifts and courage. This month is an invitation for women to recognize and celebrate the unique gifts that God has placed within each of us, while also stepping boldly into the lives we are called to lead.

Psalm 121:7-8 assures us that "The Lord keeps you from all harm and watches over your life." This promise reminds us of God's unwavering protection as we navigate our paths. Take a moment to reflect on the gifts you possess—whether they are talents, insights, or passions—and consider how they can be used to bless others and glorify God.

James 1:17 teaches us that "Whatever is good and perfect is a gift coming down to us from God." This month, let's commit to actively recognizing these gifts in our lives. From the warmth of a friend's smile to the strength we find in challenging times, these blessings can inspire us to be more grateful and generous. Share your gifts with those around you, knowing that they are part of God's perfect plan.

Courage is often required to step into our calling, and Isaiah 41:10 reassures us, "Don't be afraid, for I am with you." Embrace this courage as you take steps forward, even when uncertainty looms. Whether it's pursuing a new opportunity, standing up for what you believe in, or simply being vulnerable in relationships, remember that God walks beside you every step of the way.

Psalm 119:50 states, "Your promise revives me; it comforts me in all my troubles." Let the truth of God's promises strengthen your resolve. When doubts arise or fear threatens to hold you back, turn to His word for comfort and encouragement. Your courage can become a source of inspiration to other women around you, showing them the power of faith in action.

This month, let's also focus on supporting each other in our journeys. Romans 15:5-6 encourages us to live in harmony, fostering an environment where we can lift one another up. Share your struggles and victories with your sisters in Christ, creating a safe space for encouragement and mutual support.

At the end of July, take time to journal your reflections on the gifts you've discovered and the courage you've embraced. Celebrate the ways you've stepped out in faith and how you've witnessed God's hand at work in your life and the lives of others.

May this month be a beautiful journey of recognizing our divine gifts and stepping forward in courage, knowing that we are loved, supported, and empowered by our Creator!

July

♥ ─── ♥

1. Proverbs 18:15 - "Intelligent people are always ready to learn. Their ears are open for knowledge."

2. Psalm 121:7-8 - "The Lord keeps you from all harm and watches over your life. The Lord keeps watch over you as you come and go, both now and forever."

3. James 1:17 - "Whatever is good and perfect is a gift coming down to us from God our Father, who created all the lights in the heavens."

4. Isaiah 40:29 - "He gives power to the weak and strength to the powerless."

5. Psalm 119:32 - "I will run in the path of your commands, for you have set my heart free."

6. Proverbs 3:6 - "Seek his will in all you do, and he will show you which path to take."

7. Romans 5:1-2 - "Therefore, since we have been made right in God's sight by faith, we have peace with God because of what Jesus Christ our Lord has done for us."

8. Colossians 3:15 - "And let the peace that comes from Christ rule in your hearts. For as members of one body you are called to live in peace. And always be thankful."

9. Psalm 119:50 - "Your promise revives me; it comforts me in all my troubles."

10. 2 Timothy 2:13 - "If we are unfaithful, he remains faithful, for he cannot deny who he is."

11. Isaiah 41:10- "Don't be afraid, for I am with you. Don't be discouraged, for I am your God."

July

♥ ♥

12. Romans 15:5-6 - "May God, who gives this patience and encouragement, help you live in complete harmony with each other, as is fitting for followers of Christ Jesus."

13. Proverbs 4:7 - "Getting wisdom is the most important thing you can do! And whatever else you do, develop good judgment."

14. Philippians 4:7 - "Then you will experience God's peace, which exceeds anything we can understand."

15. Psalm 34:4 - "I prayed to the Lord, and he answered me. He freed me from all my fears."

16. Hebrews 13:5-6 - "Don't love money; be satisfied with what you have. For God has said, 'I will never fail you. I will never abandon you.'"

17. Matthew 19:26 - "Jesus looked at them intently and said, 'Humanly speaking, it is impossible. But with God everything is possible.'"

18. 1 Thessalonians 4:13-14 - "And now, dear brothers and sisters, we want you to know what will happen to the Christians who have died so you will not grieve like people who have no hope."

19. Ephesians 2:10 - "For we are God's masterpiece. He has created us anew in Christ Jesus, so we can do the good things he planned for us long ago."

20. Isaiah 58:9 - "Then when you call, the Lord will answer. 'Yes, I am here,' he will quickly reply."

21. James 1:12 - "God blesses those who patiently endure testing and temptation. Afterward they will receive the crown of life that God has promised to those who love him."

22. Philippians 2:3-4 - "Don't be selfish; don't try to impress others. Be humble, thinking of others as better than yourselves."

23. Psalm 23:4 - "Even when I walk through the darkest valley, I will not be afraid, for you are close beside me."

24. Proverbs 15:13 - "A glad heart makes a happy face; a broken heart crushes the spirit."

25. Romans 8:1 - "So now there is no condemnation for those who belong to Christ Jesus."

26. 1 Peter 3:15 - "Instead, you must worship Christ as Lord of your life. And if someone asks about your Christian hope, always be ready to explain it."

27. 2 Corinthians 1:3-4 - "All praise to God, the Father of our Lord Jesus Christ. God is our merciful Father and the source of all comfort. He comforts us in all our troubles."

28. Psalm 91:1-2 - "Those who live in the secret place of the Most High will find rest in the shadow of the Almighty."

29. Colossians 1:27 - "For God wanted them to know that the riches and glory of Christ are for you Gentiles, too. And this is the secret: Christ lives in you. This gives you assurance of sharing his glory."

30. Philippians 3:20 - "But we are citizens of heaven, where the Lord Jesus Christ lives. And we are eagerly waiting for him to return as our Savior."

31. Ephesians 6:12 - "For we are not fighting against flesh-and-blood enemies, but against evil rulers and authorities of the unseen world, against mighty powers in this dark world, and against evil spirits in the heavenly places."

Reflections

Take a moment to reflect on this months scripture. What message or messages resonate with you? How can you apply these teaching in your life today? Consider its impact on your thoughts, actions, and relationships.

––––– ♥ ––––– ♥ –––––

August

Living Authentically in God's Light

––––– ♥ ––––– ♥ –––––

Prayer Prompt:
"God, help me to live
authentically and in
alignment with your truth.
May my life reflect your
light and love in all that I
do."

Living Authentically in God's Light

As we step into August, let's embrace the theme of living authentically in God's light. This month, we are encouraged to reflect on who we truly are in Christ and how we can shine our light in a world that often seeks to dim it.

Proverbs 18:15 tells us, "Intelligent people are always ready to learn." This serves as a reminder to remain open and receptive to growth and understanding, not just about the world, but about ourselves. Spend time this month seeking knowledge that nurtures your spirit and aligns with your true self. Engage with Scripture, explore new interests, and deepen your understanding of your unique identity as a woman of God.

Psalm 121:7-8 reassures us that "The Lord keeps you from all harm and watches over your life." Recognize that you are protected and cherished by God. Embrace this security as you pursue authenticity in your relationships and actions. Knowing you are watched over, allow yourself to be vulnerable and genuine. Share your story, your struggles, and your triumphs, inviting others to see the beautiful work God is doing in you.

In Isaiah 40:29, we learn that "He gives power to the weak and strength to the powerless." This verse is a call to honor our weaknesses and turn them into strengths through God's grace. As you embrace your authentic self, remember that it's okay to ask for help and support. Share your burdens with your sisters in Christ; together, you can uplift one another and celebrate the strength that comes from community.

This month also encourages us to live out our faith actively. Matthew 5:16 says, "Let your good deeds shine out for all to see." Consider how your actions can reflect your authentic self and God's love. Look for opportunities to serve and uplift others in your daily life, making your light shine brightly. Your authenticity can inspire others to be real and honest in their own journeys.

August

As you move through August, remember the promise in Romans 8:28: "God causes everything to work together for the good of those who love Him." Even when challenges arise, trust that God is weaving your experiences into a beautiful tapestry of purpose and impact.

At the end of the month, take time to reflect on how you have embraced authenticity. What new insights have you gained about yourself? How have your actions reflected your faith? Let these reflections guide you as you continue to live authentically, shining brightly in the world and inviting others to do the same.

May this month be a celebration of the unique and beautiful women God has created us to be!

1. Proverbs 18:15 - "Intelligent people are always ready to learn. Their ears are open for knowledge."

2. Psalm 121:7-8 - "The Lord keeps you from all harm and watches over your life. The Lord keeps watch over you as you come and go, both now and forever."

3. James 1:17 - "Whatever is good and perfect is a gift coming down to us from God our Father, who created all the lights in the heavens."

4. Isaiah 40:29 - "He gives power to the weak and strength to the powerless."

5. Psalm 119:32 - "I will run in the path of your commands, for you have set my heart free."

6. Proverbs 3:6 - "Seek his will in all you do, and he will show you which path to take."

7. Romans 5:1-2 - "Therefore, since we have been made right in God's sight by faith, we have peace with God because of what Jesus Christ our Lord has done for us."

8. Colossians 3:15 - "And let the peace that comes from Christ rule in your hearts. For as members of one body you are called to live in peace. And always be thankful."

9. Psalm 119:50 - "Your promise revives me; it comforts me in all my troubles."

10. 2 Timothy 2:13 - "If we are unfaithful, he remains faithful, for he cannot deny who he is."

11. Isaiah 41:10 - "Don't be afraid, for I am with you. Don't be discouraged, for I am your God."

12. Romans 15:5-6 - "May God, who gives this patience and encouragement, help you live in complete harmony with each other, as is fitting for followers of Christ Jesus."

13. Proverbs 4:7 - "Getting wisdom is the most important thing you can do! And whatever else you do, develop good judgment."

14. Philippians 4:19 - "And this same God who takes care of me will supply all your needs from his glorious riches, which have been given to us in Christ Jesus."

15. 1 Corinthians 10:13 - "The temptations in your life are no different from what others experience. And God is faithful. He will not allow the temptation to be more than you can stand."

16. Hebrews 10:24-25 - "Let us think of ways to motivate one another to acts of love and good works. And let us not neglect our meeting together, as some people do, but encourage one another."

17. Psalm 46:1 - "God is our refuge and strength, always ready to help in times of trouble."

18. John 16:33 - "I have told you all this so that you may have peace in me. Here on earth you will have many trials and sorrows. But take heart, because I have overcome the world."

19. Matthew 5:16 - "In the same way, let your good deeds shine out for all to see, so that everyone will praise your heavenly Father."

20. Romans 8:28 - "And we know that God causes everything to work together for the good of those who love God and are called according to his purpose for them."

21. Philippians 1:6 - "And I am certain that God, who began the good work within you, will continue his work until it is finally finished on the day when Christ Jesus returns."

22. 2 Corinthians 5:17 - "This means that anyone who belongs to Christ has become a new person. The old life is gone; a new life has begun!"

23. Ephesians 4:32 - "Instead, be kind to each other, tenderhearted, forgiving one another, just as God through Christ has forgiven you."

24. Galatians 6:9 - "So let's not get tired of doing what is good. At just the right time we will reap a harvest of blessing if we don't give up."

25. Romans 12:2 - "Don't copy the behavior and customs of this world, but let God transform you into a new person by changing the way you think."

26. John 14:27 - "I am leaving you with a gift—peace of mind and heart. And the peace I give is a gift the world cannot give. So don't be troubled or afraid."

27. 1 John 4:19 - "We love each other because he loved us first."

28. Psalm 30:5 - "For his anger lasts only a moment, but his favor lasts a lifetime! Weeping may last through the night, but joy comes with the morning."

29. Proverbs 16:24 - "Kind words are like honey—sweet to the soul and healthy for the body."

30. Isaiah 41:13 - "For I hold you by your right hand—I, the Lord your God. And I say to you, 'Don't be afraid. I am here to help you.'"

Reflections

Take a moment to reflect on this months scripture. What message or messages resonate with you? How can you apply these teaching in your life today? Consider its impact on your thoughts, actions, and relationships.

September

Embracing God's Comfort and Strength

Prayer Prompt:
"Lord, in times of struggle,
remind me of your comfort
and strength. Help me to
lean on you and find solace
in your presence."

September

♥ ———— ♥

Embracing God's Comfort and Strength

As we enter September, let's embrace the theme of embracing God's comfort and strength. This month is a beautiful opportunity for women to lean into the unwavering support and care that God offers, especially during times of transition and challenge.

1 Peter 5:7 reminds us to "give all your worries and cares to God, for he cares about you." This month, let's focus on surrendering our anxieties and uncertainties to Him. Take a moment each day to reflect on your worries and consciously place them in God's hands. He invites you to let go and trust in His loving care.

Romans 15:13 speaks to the hope that fills us completely with joy and peace. As you navigate September, seek to be a vessel of this hope. Let joy and peace radiate from your heart, even in the midst of life's challenges. Remember that your trust in God is the anchor that stabilizes you amid uncertainty.

Matthew 11:28-30 invites those who are weary to find rest in Christ. This month, prioritize your well-being by setting aside moments for self-care and renewal. Whether it's a quiet moment of prayer, a nature walk, or a cozy evening with a good book, make space for rest. Allow God's gentle guidance to refresh your spirit.

Psalm 139:14 beautifully reminds us of our worth: "Thank you for making me so wonderfully complex!" Embrace your uniqueness and recognize that you are a masterpiece crafted by God. Celebrate the attributes that make you who you are, and let this self-acceptance empower you to approach the world with confidence.

As you encounter challenges, remember Isaiah 43:2: "When you go through deep waters, I will be with you." God's presence is a constant source of strength. Whenever you face difficulties, turn to Him for comfort and courage. He is right there, ready to lift you up and carry you through.

September

———————— ♥ ———————— ♥ ————————

This month, cultivate a spirit of gratitude as Psalm 9:1 encourages: "I will give thanks to you, Lord, with all my heart." Take time to reflect on the blessings in your life, big and small. Keeping a gratitude journal can help you stay mindful of God's goodness and faithfulness throughout your days.

Lastly, let the words of Lamentations 3:22-23 resonate in your heart: "The faithful love of the Lord never ends! His mercies never cease." Each day is a new beginning, filled with fresh mercies. As you step into September, embrace this truth and allow it to fill you with hope and strength.

May this month be one of deep comfort, renewed strength, and the joyful realization that you are never alone. Trust in God's unfailing love as you navigate each day, and let His light shine through you.

As you reflect on this month's theme, take a moment to journal your thoughts and experiences. Write about the times you've felt God's comfort and strength in your life. What Scripture has resonated with you? How can you lean into His presence during challenging moments? Allow your journaling to be a space for gratitude, reflection, and deeper connection with God's unwavering support.

1. 1 Peter 5:7 - "Give all your worries and cares to God, for he cares about you."

2. Romans 15:13 - "I pray that God, the source of hope, will fill you completely with joy and peace because you trust in him."

3. James 4:10 - "Humble yourselves before the Lord, and he will lift you up in honor."

4. Psalm 118:24 - "This is the day the Lord has made. We will rejoice and be glad in it."

5. Matthew 11:28-30 - "Come to me, all of you who are weary and carry heavy burdens, and I will give you rest. Take my yoke upon you. Let me teach you, because I am humble and gentle at heart, and you will find rest for your souls."

6. Titus 3:4-5 - "But—when God our Savior revealed his kindness and love, he saved us, not because of the righteous things we had done, but because of his mercy."

7. 2 Thessalonians 3:16 - "Now may the Lord of peace himself give you his peace at all times and in every situation."

8. Psalm 139:14 - "Thank you for making me so wonderfully complex! Your workmanship is marvelous—how well I know it."

9. Proverbs 4:23 - "Guard your heart above all else, for it determines the course of your life."

10. Romans 12:12 - "Rejoice in our confident hope. Be patient in trouble, and keep on praying."

11. Isaiah 26:3 - "You will keep in perfect peace all who trust in you, all whose thoughts are fixed on you."

12. Philippians 4:4 - "Always be full of joy in the Lord. I say it again—rejoice!"

13. 2 Corinthians 9:8 - "And God will generously provide all you need. Then you will always have everything you need and plenty left over to share with others."

14. Psalm 112:7 - "They do not fear bad news; they confidently trust the Lord to care for them."

15. Galatians 5:22-23 - "But the fruit of the Spirit is love, joy, peace, patience, kindness, goodness, faithfulness, gentleness, self-control."

16. Ephesians 3:20 - "Now all glory to God, who is able, through his mighty power at work within us, to accomplish infinitely more than we might ask or think."

17. Matthew 6:34 - "So don't worry about tomorrow, for tomorrow will bring its own worries. Today's trouble is enough for today."

18. Isaiah 43:2 - "When you go through deep waters, I will be with you. When you go through rivers of difficulty, you will not drown."

19. Hebrews 12:1 - "Therefore, since we are surrounded by such a huge crowd of witnesses to the life of faith, let us strip off every weight that slows us down."

20. 1 Chronicles 16:11 - "Search for the Lord and for his strength; seek his face always."

21. Psalm 9:1 - "I will give thanks to you, Lord, with all my heart; I will tell of all your wonderful deeds."

22. Lamentations 3:22-23 - "The faithful love of the Lord never ends! His mercies never cease. Great is his faithfulness; his mercies begin afresh each morning."

23. Psalm 73:26 - "My health may fail, and my spirit may grow weak, but God remains the strength of my heart; he is mine forever."

24. Matthew 7:7 - "Keep on asking, and you will receive what you ask for. Keep on seeking, and you will find. Keep on knocking, and the door will be opened to you."

25. Romans 10:17 - "So faith comes from hearing, that is, hearing the Good News about Christ."

26. 1 John 3:1 - "See how very much our Father loves us, for he calls us his children, and that is what we are!"

27. Psalm 139:16 - "You saw me before I was born. Every day of my life was recorded in your book. Every moment was laid out before a single day had passed."

28. Colossians 3:2 - "Think about the things of heaven, not the things of earth."

29. Ephesians 1:4 - "Even before he made the world, God loved us and chose us in Christ to be holy and without fault in his eyes."

30. Romans 4:20-21 - "Abraham never wavered in believing God's promise. In fact, his faith grew stronger, and in this he brought glory to God."

Take a moment to reflect on this months scripture. What message or messages resonate with you? How can you apply these teaching in your life today? Consider its impact on your thoughts, actions, and relationships.

—— ♥ —— ♥ ——

October

Living With Purpose and Gratitude

—— ♥ —— ♥ ——

Prayer Prompt:
"Father, teach me to live
each day with purpose and
gratitude. Open my eyes to
the blessings around me and
help me to be thankful in all
circumstances."

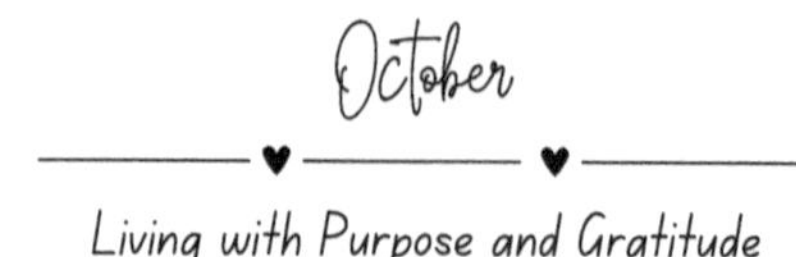

October

Living with Purpose and Gratitude

As we step into October, let's embrace the theme of living with purpose and gratitude. This month, let's focus on intentionality in our actions and cultivating a heart of thankfulness, reflecting the profound truths found in Scripture.

Philippians 2:14 reminds us to "do everything without complaining and arguing." This month, let's strive to approach our daily tasks with joy and positivity. Whether at work, home, or in our relationships, challenge yourself to find the good in every situation. Embracing gratitude can transform your perspective and deepen your sense of purpose.

2 Peter 3:9 highlights God's patience and faithfulness. As you navigate life's challenges, remember that His timing is perfect. Trust that He is working behind the scenes for your good. This month, reflect on areas where you can practice patience, whether it's in personal goals or relationships. God's timing may lead you to unexpected blessings!

James 1:5 encourages us to seek wisdom from our generous God. Make it a goal this month to intentionally ask for guidance in your decisions and interactions. Pray for wisdom in your relationships, your work, and your personal journey. When you align your choices with His will, you'll find a deeper sense of fulfillment.

Psalm 119:105 reminds us that God's Word is a lamp to our feet and a light for our path. This October, commit to spending time in Scripture. Let it guide your thoughts and actions, illuminating the way forward. As you study, you'll discover insights that empower you to live with purpose.

Isaiah 40:31 promises that those who trust in the Lord will find new strength. No matter what challenges arise this month, lean into your faith. Allow God to renew your energy and enthusiasm, enabling you to soar like eagles above your circumstances.

Incorporate gratitude into your daily routine, inspired by 1 Thessalonians 5:16-18, which

October

urges us to be thankful in all circumstances. Consider starting a gratitude journal where you note daily blessings and the ways God has been present in your life. This simple practice can shift your mindset and enhance your overall joy.

As you engage with others, remember Proverbs 27:17: "As iron sharpens iron, so a friend sharpens a friend." Surround yourself with supportive women who uplift and inspire you. This month, reach out to a friend or mentor to share your journey and encourage one another in living with purpose.

Let Psalm 103:2 inspire you: "Let all that I am praise the Lord; may I never forget the good things he does for me." Take time to reflect on God's faithfulness in your life. Celebrate His goodness, and let this gratitude fuel your actions and interactions.

This October, let's commit to living intentionally, focusing on the blessings around us, and seeking God's wisdom in every aspect of our lives. May you discover renewed purpose, deeper connections, and a heart overflowing with gratitude as you walk through this month!

Take some time to journal your thoughts, reflecting on the moments that inspire gratitude and the wisdom you encounter.

———— ♥ ———— ♥ ————

1. Philippians 2:14 - "Do everything without complaining and arguing."

2. 2 Peter 3:9 - "The Lord isn't really being slow about his promise, as some people think. No, he is being patient for your sake."

3. James 1:5 - "If you need wisdom, ask our generous God, and he will give it to you."

4. Psalm 119:105 - "Your word is a lamp to guide my feet and a light for my path."

5. Proverbs 19:21 - "You can make many plans, but the Lord's purpose will prevail."

6. Isaiah 40:31 - "But those who trust in the Lord will find new strength. They will soar high on wings like eagles."

7. Matthew 28:20 - "And be sure of this: I am with you always, even to the end of the age."

8. John 3:16 - "For God loved the world so much that he gave his one and only Son, so that everyone who believes in him will not perish but have eternal life."

9. Psalm 16:11 - "You will show me the way of life, granting me the joy of your presence and the pleasures of living with you forever."

10. 2 Corinthians 1:20** - "For all of God's promises have been fulfilled in Christ with a resounding 'Yes!'"

11. 1 Thessalonians 5:16-18** - "Always be joyful. Never stop praying. Be thankful in all circumstances, for this is God's will for you who belong to Christ Jesus."

12. John 10:10 - "The thief's purpose is to steal and kill and destroy. My purpose is to give them a rich and satisfying life."

——————— ♥ ——————— ♥ ———————

13. Psalm 55:22 - "Give your burdens to the Lord, and he will take care of you."

14. Proverbs 27:17 - "As iron sharpens iron, so a friend sharpens a friend."

15. Isaiah 26:4 - "Trust in the Lord always, for the Lord God is the eternal Rock."

16. Romans 6:23 - "For the wages of sin is death, but the free gift of God is eternal life through Christ Jesus our Lord."

17. Psalm 103:2 - "Let all that I am praise the Lord; may I never forget the good things he does for me."

18. Colossians 3:23 - "Work willingly at whatever you do, as though you were working for the Lord rather than for people."

19. I Timothy 6:12 - "Fight the good fight for the true faith. Hold tightly to the eternal life to which God has called you."

20. Psalm 37:4 - "Take delight in the Lord, and he will give you your heart's desires."

21. Isaiah 43:18-19 - "But forget all that—it is nothing compared to what I am going to do. For I am about to do something new."

22. Romans 12:1 - "And so, dear brothers and sisters, I plead with you to give your bodies to God because of all he has done for you."

23. Philippians 3:14 - "I press on to reach the end of the race and receive the heavenly prize for which God, through Christ Jesus, is calling us."

—————— ♥ —————— ♥ ——————

24. Proverbs 15:1 - "A gentle answer deflects anger, but harsh words make tempers flare."

25. 2 Samuel 22:31 - "God's way is perfect. All the Lord's promises prove true."

26. Psalm 118:6 - "The Lord is for me, so I will have no fear. What can mere people do to me?"

27. Philippians 1:3-5 - "Every time I think of you, I give thanks to my God. Whenever I pray, I make my requests for all of you with joy."

28. 1 Chronicles 29:11 - "Yours, O Lord, is the greatness, the power, the glory, the victory, and the majesty."

29. Proverbs 10:12 - "Hatred stirs up quarrels, but love makes up for all offenses."

30. Psalm 56:3 - "But when I am afraid, I will put my trust in you."

31. Isaiah 54:10 - "For the mountains may depart and the hills be removed, but my steadfast love shall not depart from you."

Reflections

Take a moment to reflect on this months scripture. What message or messages resonate with you? How can you apply these teaching in your life today? Consider its impact on your thoughts, actions, and relationships.

----- ♥ ----- ♥ -----

November

Embracing Faith and Resilience

----- ♥ ----- ♥ -----

Prayer Prompt:
"Father, teach me to live
each day with purpose and
gratitude. Open my eyes to
the blessings around me and
help me to be thankful in all
circumstances."

November

♥ —————— ♥

Embracing Faith and Resilience

As we enter November, let's focus on embracing faith and resilience. This month, we encourage you to cultivate a spirit that is steadfast in faith and strong in the face of challenges, drawing from the rich wisdom found in Scripture.

2 Corinthians 4:16 reminds us that while our bodies may face weariness, our spirits are being renewed daily. Embrace this truth! Each day is an opportunity for spiritual renewal. When you feel overwhelmed, remember that your inner strength can flourish, regardless of external circumstances.

1 Peter 1:8-9 speaks to the profound joy that comes from trusting in God, even when we can't see His plan unfolding. Let this be a reminder to celebrate your faith and the joy it brings, even amidst uncertainty. This month, actively seek moments to rejoice in your trust in Him. Reflect on the blessings in your life and allow that joy to be a light for others.

Hebrews 13:8 reassures us that Jesus remains the same—yesterday, today, and forever. In a world of change, find comfort in His unchanging nature. Let this truth anchor you as you face life's ups and downs. Write down specific instances where you've seen God's faithfulness in your life, and revisit them whenever you need encouragement.

Proverbs 3:5-6 calls us to trust in the Lord wholeheartedly. Take this month to seek His will in every decision you make. Whether it's in your personal life, career, or relationships, ask God to guide your path. By leaning on Him rather than your understanding, you will uncover a deeper purpose in your journey.

In moments of doubt, remember Philippians 4:8: fix your thoughts on what is true, honorable, and lovely. This practice can transform your mindset. Spend some time this month reflecting on these blessings in the reflections section to help you stay focused on the positive, nurturing resilience in your heart.

November

Psalm 145:18 assures us that the Lord is close to those who call on Him. This month, don't hesitate to reach out to God in prayer. Whether you're facing difficulties or simply seeking connection, approach Him boldly, knowing that He is ready to offer you grace and mercy.

Romans 8:31 powerfully proclaims that if God is for us, who can be against us? Carry this assurance in your heart as you navigate any challenges this month. Stand firm in your faith and remind yourself of the victories God has already brought you through.

Lastly, James 5:16 encourages us to pray for one another. As you embrace faith and resilience this month, connect with other women in your community. Share your struggles and victories, pray together, and uplift each other. In unity, you'll find strength and encouragement.

Take some time to reflect. Write about moments where you felt God's presence, instances of joy, or challenges you faced and how your faith helped you navigate them. Let this practice deepen your understanding of His faithfulness and inspire resilience in your journey.

Let November be a time of deepening faith and growing resilience. Embrace each day with the knowledge that God is with you, renewing your spirit and guiding your path. As you trust in Him and lean into community, may you experience the richness of His presence in every moment.

———————— ♥ ———————— ♥ ————————

1. 2 Corinthians 4:16 - "That is why we never give up. Though our bodies are dying, our spirits are being renewed every day."

2. Hebrews 4:16 - "So let us come boldly to the throne of our gracious God. There we will receive his mercy, and we will find grace to help us when we need it most."

3. Philippians 4:8 - "And now, dear brothers and sisters, one final thing. Fix your thoughts on what is true, and honorable, and right, and pure, and lovely, and admirable."

4. Psalm 145:18 - "The Lord is close to all who call on him, yes, to all who call on him in truth."

5. John 14:6 - "Jesus told him, 'I am the way, the truth, and the life. No one can come to the Father except through me.'"

6. Ephesians 1:7 - "He is so rich in kindness and grace that he purchased our freedom with the blood of his Son and forgave our sins."

7. Psalm 37:5 - "Commit everything you do to the Lord. Trust him, and he will help you."

8. Romans 8:31 - "What shall we say about such wonderful things as these? If God is for us, who can ever be against us?"

9. Isaiah 40:11 - "He will feed his flock like a shepherd. He will carry the lambs in his arms, holding them close to his heart."

10. James 5:16 - "Confess your sins to each other and pray for each other so that you may be healed."

11. Psalm 34:8 - "Taste and see that the Lord is good. Oh, the joys of those who take refuge in him!"

———————— ♥ ———————— ♥ ————————

12. 1 Peter 1:8-9 - "You love him even though you have never seen him. Though you do not see him now, you trust him; and you rejoice with a glorious, inexpressible joy."

13. Hebrews 13:8 - "Jesus Christ is the same yesterday, today, and forever."

14. Proverbs 3:5-6 - "Trust in the Lord with all your heart; do not depend on your own understanding. Seek his will in all you do, and he will show you which path to take."

15. 1 John 5:14 - "And we are confident that he hears us whenever we ask for anything that pleases him."

16. Psalm 25:4-5 - "Show me your ways, Lord; teach me your paths. Guide me in your truth and teach me, for you are God my Savior, and my hope is in you all day long."

17. John 15:5 - "Yes, I am the vine; you are the branches. Those who remain in me, and I in them, will produce much fruit. For apart from me you can do nothing."

18. Psalm 112:1 - "Praise the Lord! How joyful are those who fear the Lord and delight in obeying his commands."

19. Romans 1:17 - "For in it the righteousness of God is revealed from faith for faith, as it is written, 'The righteous shall live by faith.'"

20. Philippians 2:14-15 - "Do everything without complaining and arguing, so that no one can criticize you. Live clean, innocent lives as children of God."

21. Proverbs 11:25 - "The generous will prosper; those who refresh others will themselves be refreshed."

22. Psalm 139:7-10 - "I can never escape from your Spirit! I can never get away from your presence!"

———— ♥ ———— ♥ ————

23. 2 Corinthians 12:9 - "But he said to me, 'My grace is sufficient for you, for my power is made perfect in weakness.'"

24. Matthew 6:33 - "Seek the Kingdom of God above all else, and live righteously, and he will give you everything you need."

25. Hebrews 11:1 - "Faith shows the reality of what we hope for; it is the evidence of things we cannot see."

26. Romans 12:21 - "Don't let evil conquer you, but conquer evil by doing good."

27. Proverbs 14:30 - "A peaceful heart leads to a healthy body; jealousy is like cancer in the bones."

28. Psalm 116:1-2 - "I love the Lord because he hears my voice and my prayer for mercy. Because he bends down to listen, I will pray as long as I have breath."

29. 1 Timothy 1:14 - "Oh, how generous and gracious our Lord was! He filled me with the faith and love that come from Christ Jesus."

29. Isaiah 32:17 - "And this righteousness will bring peace. Yes, it will bring quietness and confidence forever."

30. Psalm 91:11 - "For he will order his angels to protect you wherever you go."

Reflections

Take a moment to reflect on this months scripture. What message or messages resonate with you? How can you apply these teaching in your life today? Consider its impact on your thoughts, actions, and relationships.

---- ♥ ---- ♥ ----

December

Radiating Love and Purpose

---- ♥ ---- ♥ ----

Prayer Prompt:
"Lord, help me to radiate
your love and purpose in this
season. May my actions
reflect your grace, bringing
joy to those around me."

December

Radiating Love and Purpose

As we step into December, let's focus on radiating love and purpose. This month, we're called to embrace the incredible light within us and share it with the world, drawing strength and guidance from Scripture.

Matthew 5:14 reminds us that we are the light of the world—a beacon of hope and love. Embrace your role as a source of light for those around you. Each small act of kindness, encouragement, or support can illuminate someone's path, reflecting God's love through you.

Drawing near to God, as stated in James 4:8, opens our hearts to His presence and guidance. This month, prioritize spending time in His Word and in prayer. Allow Him to fill you with His love so that you can share it abundantly with others.

Philippians 3:13-14 encourages us to forget the past and look forward to what lies ahead. Let this be a time of letting go of burdens that weigh you down and embracing the possibilities that God has for you. Write down any past hurts or regrets in your journal, and then symbolically release them, focusing instead on your goals and dreams.

In 1 John 4:16, we're reminded that God is love. As you draw nearer to Him, let His love fill you and overflow into your relationships. Reflect on how you can express that love to those around you. This could be through simple gestures of kindness or deeper acts of service.

Proverbs 2:6 tells us that wisdom comes from the Lord. This month, seek His wisdom in every decision you face. Journal your prayers asking for guidance, and take note of how He leads you. Your trust in His wisdom will not only strengthen you but will also empower those around you.

As you encounter challenges, remember 2 Timothy 1:7, which assures us that God gives us a spirit of power, love, and self-discipline. Embrace this strength as you tackle daily tasks, knowing that you are equipped for whatever comes your way. Psalm 121:2 reminds us that our help comes from the Lord. When you feel overwhelmed, take a moment to pause and pray, seeking His assistance. Trust that He is your support and source of strength.

Journaling Prompt: Throughout this month, reflect in your journal on how you've experienced God's love and guidance. Write about moments when you've acted as a light for others or when someone's love has impacted you. Consider what it means to live with purpose and how you can actively seek to radiate that love in your daily life.

Let this December be a time to shine brightly, love deeply, and pursue the purpose God has for you. As you reflect His light and love, you will inspire others to do the same, creating a ripple effect of kindness and joy. Embrace the opportunity to grow in your faith and make a meaningful impact in the lives of those around you.

December

♥ —— ♥

1. Matthew 5:14 - "You are the light of the world—like a city on a hilltop that cannot be hidden."

2. James 4:8 - "Draw near to God, and he will draw near to you."

3. 2 Corinthians 5:7 - "For we walk by faith, not by sight."

4. Philippians 3:13-14 - "No, dear brothers and sisters, I have not achieved it, but I focus on this one thing: Forgetting the past and looking forward to what lies ahead."

5. 1 John 4:16 - "So we have come to know and to believe the love that God has for us. God is love, and whoever abides in love abides in God, and God abides in them."

6. Proverbs 2:6 - "For the Lord grants wisdom! From his mouth come knowledge and understanding."

7. Psalm 127:2 - "It is useless for you to work so hard from early morning until late at night, anxiously working for food to eat; for God gives rest to his loved ones."

8. Matthew 22:39 - "A second is equally important: 'Love your neighbor as yourself.'"

9. 1 Peter 2:9 - "But you are not like that, for you are a chosen people. You are royal priests, a holy nation, God's very own possession."

10. Isaiah 26:12 - "Lord, you will grant us peace; all we have accomplished is really from you."

11. 2 Timothy 1:7 - "For God has not given us a spirit of fear and timidity, but of power, love, and self-discipline."

——————— ♥ ——————— ♥ ———————

12. Psalm 1:2-3 - "But they delight in the law of the Lord, meditating on it day and night. They are like trees planted along the riverbank, bearing fruit each season."

13. Proverbs 3:24 - "You can go to bed without fear; you will lie down and sleep soundly."

14. Hebrews 10:23 - "Let us hold tightly without wavering to the hope we affirm, for God can be trusted to keep his promise."

15. 1 Thessalonians 4:11-12 - "Make it your goal to live a quiet life, minding your own business and working with your hands."

16. Psalm 121:2 - "My help comes from the Lord, who made heaven and earth!"

17. Isaiah 55:12 - "You will go out in joy and be led forth in peace; the mountains and hills will burst into song before you."

18. Luke 6:31 - "Do to others as you would like them to do to you."

19. Romans 12:3 - "Because of the privilege and authority God has given me, I give each of you this warning: Don't think you are better than you really are."

20. 1 John 1:9 - "If we confess our sins, he is faithful and just to forgive us our sins and to cleanse us from all wickedness."

21. Philippians 4:13 - "For I can do everything through Christ, who gives me strength."

22. Psalm 119:11 - "I have hidden your word in my heart, that I might not sin against you."

23. Proverbs 15:30 - "A cheerful look brings joy to the heart; good news makes for good health."

24. Isaiah 40:29-31 - "He gives power to the weak and strength to the powerless. Even youths will become weak and tired, and young men will fall in exhaustion. But those who trust in the Lord will find new strength."

25. Matthew 7:12 - "Do to others whatever you would like them to do to you."

26. Romans 8:32 - "Since he did not spare even his own Son but gave him up for us all, won't he also give us everything else?"

27. James 1:22 - "But don't just listen to God's word. You must do what it says. Otherwise, you are only fooling yourselves."

28. 2 Chronicles 20:17 - "You will not need to fight in this battle. Position yourselves, stand still and see the salvation of the Lord."

29. Hebrews 12:2 - "We do this by keeping our eyes on Jesus, the champion who initiates and perfects our faith."

30. Psalm 119:114 - "You are my refuge and my shield; your word is my source of hope."

31. 1 Thessalonians 5:18 - "Be thankful in all circumstances, for this is God's will for you who belong the Christ Jesus."

Take a moment to reflect on this months scripture. What message or messages resonate with you? How can you apply these teaching in your life today? Consider its impact on your thoughts, actions, and relationships.

Thank You

———— ♥ ———— ♥ ————

As we conclude this journey through "Grace Filled Days", I want to extend my heartfelt gratitude to you for embarking on this transformative path. Your commitment to embracing grace—both for yourself and others—reflects the spirit of love and kindness we aim to cultivate.

Throughout our time together, we've explored themes of renewal, peace, community, growth, and the power of living authentically. Each daily verse and reflection has been designed to uplift and inspire, reminding us of the profound wisdom found in Scripture.

May you carry the light of grace into your daily life, sharing it generously with those around you. Thank you for allowing this book to be part of your journey. Remember, every day is an opportunity to radiate love and purpose, enriching both your life and the lives of others.

With heartfelt gratitude,
Jaclyn

Additional Resources

To deepen your understanding, consider exploring these books and resources:

- The Purpose Driven Life by Rick Warren
- Jesus Calling by Sarah Young
- Mere Christianity by C.S. Lewis

Prayer Resources

- Books on Prayer:
  - The Power of a Praying Wife by Stormie Omartian
  - Prayer: Experiencing Awe and Intimacy with God by Timothy Keller
- Online Resources:
  - www.prayer.com - A platform for prayer requests and community support.
  - www.theprayerproject.com - Daily prayer prompts and resources.

Reflection Journals

- The One Year Prayer Journal - A structured journal for daily prayer and reflection.
- Gratitude Journal - A space to document daily blessings and insights.

Community and Support

- Bible Study Groups:
  - Join or start a local Bible study group to share insights and encourage one another.
  - Online groups and forums, such as those found on platforms like Facebook or Meetup.
- Church Resources:
  - Check with your local church for study groups, prayer circles, or counseling services.

Apps for Daily Inspiration

- YouVersion Bible App: Offers daily verses, plans, and community features.
- Pray as You Go: A daily prayer app that combines music, scripture, and reflection.

Recommended Bible Versions

- New Living Translation (NLT): The version used in this book for its readability and contemporary language.
- English Standard Version (ESV): A more literal translation for deeper study.

www.ingramcontent.com/pod-product-compliance
Lightning Source LLC
Chambersburg PA
CBHW040151160726
48006CB00014B/1706